ANIMAL SECRETS

Deborah Underwood

Raintree

www.raintreepublishers.co.uk
Visit our website to find out more information about **Raintree** books.

To order:
 Phone 44 (0) 1865 888112
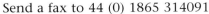 Send a fax to 44 (0) 1865 314091
 Visit the Raintree Bookshop at **www.raintreepublishers.co.uk** to browse
our catalogue and order online.

First published in Great Britain by Raintree,
Halley Court, Jordan Hill, Oxford OX2 8EJ,
part of Harcourt Education.
Raintree is a registered trademark of Harcourt
Education Ltd.

© Harcourt Education Ltd 2008
First published in paperback in 2008
The moral right of the proprietor has been asserted.

Editorial: Nancy Dickmann and Catherine Veitch
Design: Philippa Jenkins and Q2A Creative
Picture Research: Ruth Blair
Production: Alison Parsons

Originated by Modern Age
Printed and bound in China by Leo Paper Group

ISBN 978 1 4062 0731 6 (hardback)
12 11 10 09 08
10 9 8 7 6 5 4 3 2 1

ISBN 978 1 4062 0745 3 (paperback)
12 11 10 09 08
10 9 8 7 6 5 4 3 2 1

**British Library Cataloguing in Publication
Data**
Underwood, Deborah
Animal secrets. - (Fusion)
1. Animals - Adaptation - Juvenile literature
2. Physiology - Juvenile literature
I. Title 591.4
A full catalogue record for this book is available from
the British Library.

Acknowledgements
The author and publisher are grateful to the
following for permission to reproduce copyright
material: FLPA (Minden Pictures) p.**13** (Mitsuhiko
Imamori), **26** (Patricio Robles Gil, Sierra Madre);
Naturepl.com p.**9** (Staffan Widstrand), **23** (Phil
Savole), **27** (Reinhard/ARCO); NHPA pp.**4-5** (Martin
Harvey), **7** (Robert Erwin), **12** (Nobert Wu), **17**
(Michael Leach), **20** (Stephen Dalton); OSF p.**25**
(Rudie Kuiter); Oxford Scientific pp.**28-29** (Stan
Osolinski); Photolibrary.com p.**8** (Peter Lillie), **10-
11** (Monsoon Images), **15** (Pacific Stock), **18-19**
(Workbookstock, Inc), **21** (Mauritius Images), **22**
(Animals Animals; Earth Scenes).

Cover photograph of basilisk lizard running on water
reproduced with permission of Photolibrary.com.

Every effort has been made to contact copyright
holders of any material reproduced in this book. Any
omissions will be rectified in subsequent printings if
notice is given to the publishers.

The publishers would like to thank Nancy Harris and
Harold Pratt for their assistance with the preparation
of this book.

Disclaimer
All the Internet addresses (URLs) given in this book
were valid at the time of going to press. However,
due to the dynamic nature of the Internet, some
addresses may have changed, or sites may have
changed or ceased to exist since publication. While
the author and publishers regret any inconvenience
this may cause readers, no responsibility for any
such changes can be accepted by either the author
or the publishers.

It is recommended that adults supervise children on
the Internet.

Contents

Some words are printed in bold, **like this**. You can find out what they mean on page 30. You can also look in the box at the bottom of the page where they first appear.

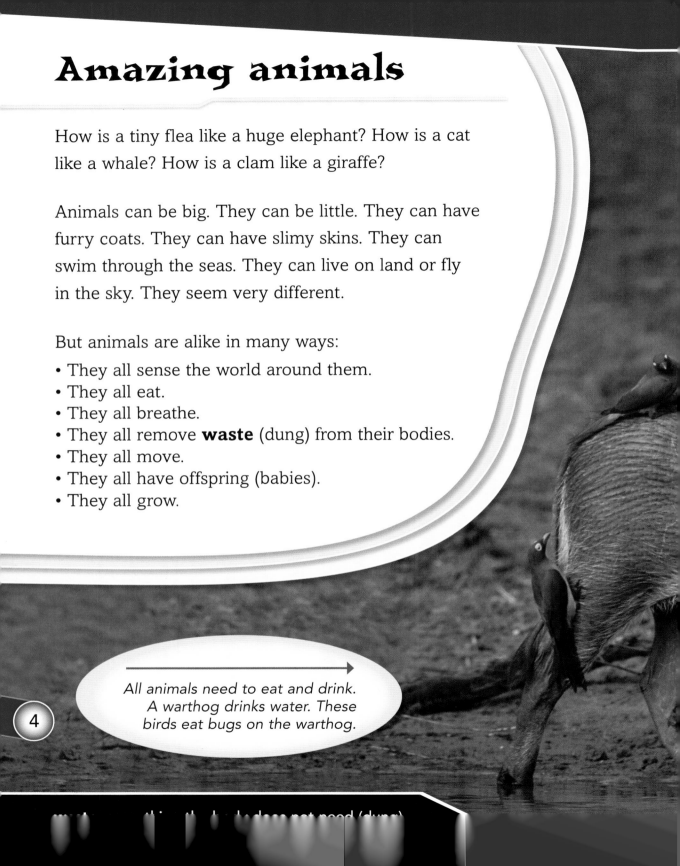

Amazing animals

How is a tiny flea like a huge elephant? How is a cat like a whale? How is a clam like a giraffe?

Animals can be big. They can be little. They can have furry coats. They can have slimy skins. They can swim through the seas. They can live on land or fly in the sky. They seem very different.

But animals are alike in many ways:

- They all sense the world around them.
- They all eat.
- They all breathe.
- They all remove **waste** (dung) from their bodies.
- They all move.
- They all have offspring (babies).
- They all grow.

All animals need to eat and drink. A warthog drinks water. These birds eat bugs on the warthog.

How do animals do these things? The answers may surprise you. Amazing things happen inside all animals. You cannot tell just by looking at them. Let's find out!

Animal senses

A butterfly lands on a plant. She tastes it. But she does not use her mouth. Butterflies taste with their feet!

All animals **sense** the world around them. A dog sniffs to find food. A bird looks for a safe place to land. A cat listens for strange noises.

Animals find out about the world by using their senses. Many animals have five senses. These are sight, hearing, smell, touch, and taste.

Hawks have great eyesight. This helps them hunt. A hawk spots small animals from the air. Then the hawk swoops down for a meal.

Some animals have special senses. A rattlesnake can sense if a warm animal is close by. The snake has two pits on its face. The pits sense tiny changes in temperature. This lets the snake hunt in the dark.

Super smeller award

The male emperor moth can smell a female moth more than 10 kilometres (6 miles) away!

Hawks can see eight times better than humans can.

Grub's up!

What do all animals need? Look in your fridge for a hint. All living things need food. The food gives them **energy**. Energy is what lets their bodies do work. Plants make their own food. But animals must eat.

Not all animals need to eat meat to be strong. Just ask an elephant! Elephants are **herbivores**. They eat only plants. An African elephant can eat almost 300 kilograms (700 pounds) of plants in one day. Many herbivores spend a lot of their time eating.

Elephants use their trunks to reach leaves high up in the trees.

Koalas eat the leaves from eucalyptus trees. ↓

Enormous eater award

1st

One type of caterpillar eats 86,000 times its own weight. It does this in less than two months. This would be like a human baby eating 60 elephants!

Koalas are fussy eaters. They only eat leaves from a certain type of tree. They do not get much energy from the leaves. So, they save energy. They move slowly.

Meaty meals

Some animals eat other animals. They are called **carnivores**. Carnivores must catch their food. Many can run or swim quickly. Lions and tigers are carnivores. So are seals and sea lions.

Snakes are carnivores, too. Sometimes they eat huge meals. Then they do not need to eat for a while. Some snakes can go for months without eating.

1st Big eater award

Blue whales are the biggest animals in the world. They dine on tiny shrimp-like animals. These animals are called krill. The krill are less than 8 centimetres (3 inches) long. So, the whales eat a lot of them. They can eat almost 4 tonnes (4 tons) of krill a day!

carnivore animal that eats meat

Lions have sharp teeth and claws to help them eat.

Omnivores eat meat and plants. Raccoons are omnivores. So are many birds and most bears. If plants are hard to find, they eat meat. If meat is hard to find, they eat plants.

Creepy eaters

Some animals have strange eating habits. A cookie-cutter shark is only about 50 centimetres (20 inches) long. It takes bites out of large seals and whales. The bigger animals end up with round scars.

Houseflies cannot eat solid food. They spit on food. The food softens. Then they suck it up. Sometimes they throw up food to soften it more.

Vampire bats drink other animals' blood. They can drink half their weight in blood each night.

Cookie-cutter sharks take bites out of other animals.

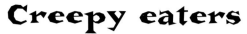

↑ Dung beetles shape dung into a ball.

Tapeworms live inside other animals. They do not need mouths or stomachs. They take in food through their skin.

13

All animals must get rid of **waste**. Liquid waste leaves the body as **urine**. Some parts of food are not used. The body gets rid of them. We call an animal's solid waste **faeces**. But a dung beetle calls it dinner!

Energy factories

All animals need **energy**. Energy lets them move. Where does energy come from?

Food breaks down into sugars. Blood carries sugars to the **cells**. Cells are like tiny building blocks that make up plants and animals.

Cells turn the sugars into energy. But they cannot do it without **oxygen**. Oxygen is part of the air we breathe.

A cell takes sugars from food. It mixes them with oxygen from the air. It turns them into energy.

When a cell makes energy, it also makes a gas called **carbon dioxide**. Carbon dioxide is **waste**. The animal breathes it out. Plants use the carbon dioxide and sunlight to make sugars again.

Dolphins breathe air like we do. They cannot breathe underwater.

carbon dioxide gas animals breathe out
cell tiny building block that makes up all living things
oxygen part of the air we breathe

1st Super sleeper award

A dolphin sleeps with half its brain at a time! The other half stays awake to breathe.

Ways to breathe

How do animals breathe? Some take air into their lungs. The lungs send **oxygen** into the blood. The blood carries the oxygen throughout the body. Bears breathe this way. So do humans.

Fish do not have lungs. They have **gills**. Water rushes into a fish's mouth when it swims. The water passes over the gills. The gills take oxygen from the water.

Many fish can pump water over their gills. That way they can breathe when they are not moving. But some sharks cannot do this. They must keep moving all the time.

Insects breathe through holes in their bodies. The holes are called **spiracles**. The spiracles connect to tubes inside the insect. Air comes in through the spiracles. It travels through the tubes. Then it goes to the rest of the body.

gill   body part that helps some sea animals take oxygen from water

These hissing cockroaches breathe through holes called spiracles. The spiracles are underneath the cockroaches.

Get moving!

Animals eat. Their bodies turn food into **energy**. Then they can move!

Cheetahs can run 113 kilometres (70 miles) an hour. Why are they so fast? Because they hunt animals that also run fast. A slow cheetah would starve.

All animals move. The main reasons they move are:
• to find food
• to find a **mate** (partner for having offspring)
• to find a place to live
• to get out of danger.

Fastest flier award

Peregrine falcons swoop down to catch other birds. They can dive at 322 kilometres (200 miles) per hour!

mate   partner for having offspring

Some animals do not move from place to place. But they still move their bodies. Most of these animals live in the sea. An adult sponge spends its life in one spot. It finds plenty to eat there. Ocean currents bring food. Imagine if bits of food blew by your mouth all day and night. You could stay in one place, too!

↑ Cheetahs are the fastest land animal.

Groovy moves

The way an animal moves depends on its home. Some monkeys are good at swinging from trees. Penguins are great swimmers. But some animals move in surprising ways.

The basilisk lizard runs on water! It zooms across water to escape danger. Scientists studied how basilisks move. That helped them make a robot that walks on water.

Basilisk lizards can run on water.

1st Giant jumper award

Spittle bugs are less than 6 millimetres (¼ inch) long. But they can jump nearly 70 centimetres (28 inches)! This would be like a pet cat jumping 53 metres (175 feet).

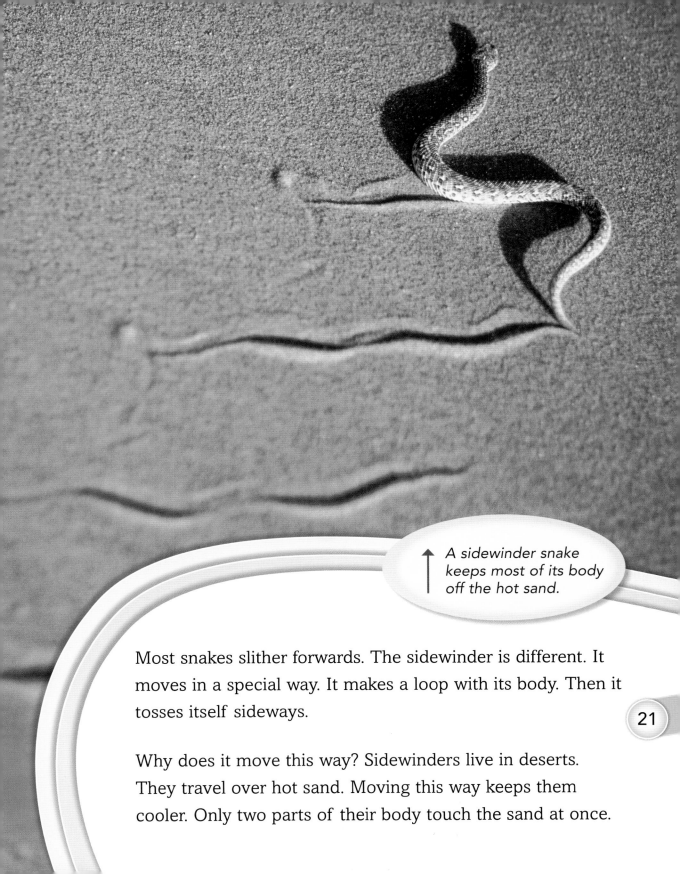

↑ A sidewinder snake keeps most of its body off the hot sand.

Most snakes slither forwards. The sidewinder is different. It moves in a special way. It makes a loop with its body. Then it tosses itself sideways.

Why does it move this way? Sidewinders live in deserts. They travel over hot sand. Moving this way keeps them cooler. Only two parts of their body touch the sand at once.

Baby talk

All animals need a way to **reproduce** (have offspring). If they did not, soon all animals would die out.

Sometimes one parent makes offspring alone. This is called **asexual reproduction**.

A planarian is a kind of flatworm. It can split into two parts. The front grows a new back. The back grows a new front. One worm becomes two.

Planarians can reproduce by splitting in two.

asexual reproduction   when an animal has offspring alone
reproduce   have offspring
sexual reproduction   when a male and female join to have offspring

All New Mexico whiptail lizards are female. Their eggs do not need sperm.

Some offspring grow on their parents. The offspring starts as a small bud. It gets bigger. Then it breaks off. It finds its own home. Some sponges reproduce this way.

Most animals need males and females to reproduce. This is called **sexual reproduction**. The female makes eggs. The male makes **cells** called **sperm**. Cells are the smallest units in living things. Eggs and sperm join together. They grow into offspring.

23

More ways to reproduce

Eggs and **sperm** may join outside the parents' bodies.
A female sunfish may lay 300 million eggs! She lays
them in the sea. The male puts sperm in the sea, too.
It is hard for the eggs and sperm to find each other.
That is one reason the female lays so many eggs.

Sometimes eggs and sperm join inside a female's body.
The female lays the eggs after they join. The eggs hatch
outside her body. This is how birds have offspring.

Some offspring grow inside a parent. We say the parent
is **pregnant**. Then the parent gives birth to the baby.
Usually the females get pregnant. But not always!
A female sea horse lays eggs in the male's body.
The male gives birth to baby sea horses.

Fabulous father award

A female emperor penguin lays one egg
in the freezing cold. The male penguin
then warms the egg on his feet.
He does this for more than two months!

*This male sea horse
is giving birth to a
tiny baby.*

Getting bigger

All offspring have a job to do. They must grow.
Sometimes they grow a lot!

Some babies change a lot as they grow. King penguin
chicks look like brown balls of fluff. Adults have sleek
black and white feathers.

Some animals change even more. A caterpillar spins
a **cocoon** (silky cover) around its body. The caterpillar
turns into a butterfly inside the cocoon. A big change
like this is called a **metamorphosis**.

Baby blue whales gain
90 kilograms (200 pounds)
every day! They weigh almost
3 tonnes (3 tons) at birth.
Females can grow to be
150 tonnes (136 tons).

cocoon silky covering
metamorphosis big change in an animal's body

Babies eat, breathe, and move. They use their **senses**. They get rid of **waste**. They grow into adults. Then they can have babies of their own.

The next time you see an animal, look closely. It may eat strange things. It may move in a weird way. You never know what secrets it may be hiding!

King penguin chicks look very different from adults.

Things all animals do

Animals look different. But they all do certain things. Look at what this greater kudu can do.

All animals grow.

All animals get rid of **waste** (something the body does not need).

All animals **reproduce** (have offspring).

All animals move. Some do not move from place to place. But they still move parts of their bodies.

All animals **sense** the world around them.

All animals make **energy** from **oxygen** and food. Energy lets the body do work.

All animals eat. They may eat plants, animals, or both.

29

Glossary

asexual reproduction when an animal has offspring alone. Sponges can have offspring using asexual reproduction.

carbon dioxide gas animals breathe out. Plants use carbon dioxide to make their food.

carnivore animal that eats meat. Carnivores have sharp teeth and claws.

cell tiny building block that makes up all living things

cocoon silky covering. A butterfly comes out of a cocoon.

energy ability to do work. You need energy to run and jump.

faeces solid waste. Food the body cannot use passes out in faeces.

gill body part that helps some sea animals take oxygen from water. Fish breathe using their gills.

herbivore animal that eats only plants. Elephants are herbivores.

mate partner for having offspring. Some animals must find mates in order to have offspring (babies).

metamorphosis big change in an animal's body. When a caterpillar turns into a butterfly, it is called metamorphosis.

omnivore animal that eats meat and plants. Omnivores can eat many types of food.

oxygen part of the air we breathe. Animals use oxygen to make energy.

pregnant has a baby growing inside. Usually the female animal gets pregnant.

reproduce have offspring. Animals reproduce in many ways.

sense ability that helps animals learn about their world. Sight and hearing are senses.

sexual reproduction when a male and female join to have offspring. Egg and sperm join in sexual reproduction.

sperm male cell that joins with an egg. A sperm and an egg combine to make a new life.

spiracle hole an insect uses to breathe. Insects usually have several spiracles.

urine liquid waste. Urine contains water and waste from cells.

waste something the body does not need (dung). Animals remove waste from their bodies.

Want to know more?

Books to read

- *Amazing Animals Q and A* (DK Publishing, 2007)

- *Animal Groups: Life in a Rookery: Penguins*, Richard and Louise Spilsbury (Heinemann Library, 2004)

- *Animals Head to Head: Lion vs. Tiger*, Isabel Thomas (Raintree, 2006)

- *Life Cycles: The Life of a Butterfly*, Clare Hibbert (Raintree, 2005)

- *National Geographic Animal Encyclopedia* (National Geographic Society, 2000)

Websites

- http://kids.nationalgeographic.com
  Learn about different animals.
- http://www.guinnessworldrecords.com/records/natural_world
  Find out about record-breaking animals.

Unearth the secrets of some amazing plants in ***Plant Secrets***.

Read about unusual partnerships in the animal world in ***You Scratch My Back***...

Index